50 Sushi Making at Home Recipes for Home

By: Kelly Johnson

Table of Contents

- Classic California Roll
- Spicy Tuna Roll
- Dragon Roll
- Rainbow Roll
- Philadelphia Roll
- Salmon Avocado Roll
- Dynamite Roll
- Spider Roll
- Tempura Shrimp Roll
- Caterpillar Roll
- Veggie Roll
- Dragonfly Roll
- Crunchy Roll
- Lobster Roll
- Teriyaki Chicken Roll
- Scallop Roll
- Volcano Roll
- Mango Tango Roll
- Hawaiian Roll
- Cucumber Roll
- Philadelphia Crunch Roll
- Soft Shell Crab Roll
- Shrimp Tempura Roll
- Unagi Roll
- Tuna Nigiri
- Salmon Nigiri
- Yellowtail Nigiri
- Eel Nigiri
- Shrimp Nigiri
- Scallop Nigiri
- Tamago Nigiri
- Octopus Nigiri
- Mackerel Nigiri
- Squid Nigiri
- Surf and Turf Roll

- Green Dragon Roll
- Rainbow Dragon Roll
- Sunrise Roll
- Sunset Roll
- Firecracker Roll
- Dynamite Crunch Roll
- Panko Crusted Roll
- Tuna Tataki Roll
- Seared Salmon Roll
- Avocado Cucumber Roll
- Tofu Roll
- Kimchi Roll
- Pickled Radish Roll
- Quinoa Roll
- Sashimi Salad Roll

Classic California Roll

Ingredients:

- 2 cups sushi rice
- 2 1/2 cups water
- 1/2 cup rice vinegar
- 2 tablespoons sugar
- 1 teaspoon salt
- 4 sheets nori seaweed
- 1 ripe avocado, sliced
- 8 ounces imitation crab meat (or cooked real crab meat), shredded
- 1 cucumber, peeled, seeded, and cut into matchsticks
- Soy sauce, for serving
- Pickled ginger, for serving
- Wasabi, for serving

Instructions:

1. Rinse the sushi rice under cold water until the water runs clear. Combine the rice and water in a rice cooker and cook according to the manufacturer's instructions. Alternatively, you can cook the rice on the stovetop by bringing it to a boil, then reducing the heat to low and simmering, covered, for about 18-20 minutes, or until the water is absorbed and the rice is tender.
2. In a small saucepan, combine the rice vinegar, sugar, and salt. Heat over medium heat until the sugar and salt are dissolved. Remove from heat and let the mixture cool.
3. Transfer the cooked rice to a large bowl and gently fold in the vinegar mixture, being careful not to mash the rice. Allow the rice to cool to room temperature.
4. Place a sheet of nori seaweed on a bamboo sushi mat, shiny side down. With wet hands, spread about 1/2 cup of sushi rice evenly over the nori, leaving a 1-inch border at the top edge.
5. Arrange slices of avocado, shredded crab meat, and cucumber matchsticks in a line across the center of the rice.
6. Using the bamboo mat, tightly roll the sushi away from you, pressing gently to seal the edge. Dampen the top edge of the nori with a little water to help it stick.
7. Repeat the process with the remaining nori sheets and ingredients.
8. Using a sharp knife dipped in water, slice each roll into 6-8 pieces.

9. Serve the California rolls with soy sauce, pickled ginger, and wasabi on the side.

Enjoy your homemade Classic California Rolls!

Spicy Tuna Roll

Ingredients:

- 2 cups sushi rice
- 2 1/2 cups water
- 1/2 cup rice vinegar
- 2 tablespoons sugar
- 1 teaspoon salt
- 4 sheets nori seaweed
- 8 ounces sushi-grade tuna, finely chopped
- 2 tablespoons mayonnaise
- 1 tablespoon Sriracha sauce (adjust to taste)
- 1 teaspoon sesame oil
- 1/2 cucumber, peeled, seeded, and cut into matchsticks
- Soy sauce, for serving
- Pickled ginger, for serving
- Wasabi, for serving
- Sesame seeds, for garnish (optional)

Instructions:

1. Rinse the sushi rice under cold water until the water runs clear. Cook the rice either in a rice cooker or on the stovetop according to the package instructions. Let it cool to room temperature.
2. In a small saucepan, combine the rice vinegar, sugar, and salt. Heat over medium heat until the sugar and salt dissolve. Remove from heat and let the mixture cool.
3. Once the rice is cooled, gently fold in the vinegar mixture until well combined. Set aside.
4. In a small bowl, mix together the chopped tuna, mayonnaise, Sriracha sauce, and sesame oil until evenly combined. Adjust the amount of Sriracha sauce according to your desired level of spiciness.
5. Place a sheet of nori seaweed on a bamboo sushi mat, shiny side down. With wet hands, spread about 1/2 cup of sushi rice evenly over the nori, leaving a 1-inch border at the top edge.
6. Spread a thin layer of the spicy tuna mixture across the center of the rice.
7. Arrange cucumber matchsticks on top of the tuna mixture.

8. Using the bamboo mat, tightly roll the sushi away from you, pressing gently to seal the edge. Dampen the top edge of the nori with a little water to help it stick.
9. Repeat the process with the remaining nori sheets and ingredients.
10. Using a sharp knife dipped in water, slice each roll into 6-8 pieces.
11. Serve the Spicy Tuna Rolls with soy sauce, pickled ginger, and wasabi on the side. Optionally, sprinkle sesame seeds on top for garnish.

Enjoy your homemade Spicy Tuna Rolls!

Dragon Roll

Ingredients:

- 2 cups sushi rice
- 2 1/2 cups water
- 1/2 cup rice vinegar
- 2 tablespoons sugar
- 1 teaspoon salt
- 4 sheets nori seaweed
- 8 ounces sushi-grade cooked shrimp, sliced in half lengthwise
- 1 ripe avocado, thinly sliced
- 1/2 cucumber, peeled, seeded, and cut into matchsticks
- 1 tablespoon mayonnaise
- 1 teaspoon Sriracha sauce
- 1 teaspoon sesame oil
- Soy sauce, for serving
- Pickled ginger, for serving
- Wasabi, for serving
- Sesame seeds, for garnish (optional)

Instructions:

1. Rinse the sushi rice under cold water until the water runs clear. Cook the rice either in a rice cooker or on the stovetop according to the package instructions. Let it cool to room temperature.
2. In a small saucepan, combine the rice vinegar, sugar, and salt. Heat over medium heat until the sugar and salt dissolve. Remove from heat and let the mixture cool.
3. Once the rice is cooled, gently fold in the vinegar mixture until well combined. Set aside.
4. In a small bowl, mix together the mayonnaise, Sriracha sauce, and sesame oil until evenly combined.
5. Place a sheet of nori seaweed on a bamboo sushi mat, shiny side down. With wet hands, spread about 1/2 cup of sushi rice evenly over the nori, leaving a 1-inch border at the top edge.
6. Spread a thin layer of the spicy mayonnaise mixture across the center of the rice.
7. Arrange slices of avocado and cucumber matchsticks on top of the spicy mayonnaise mixture.

8. Place the sliced shrimp on top of the avocado and cucumber, slightly overlapping them.
9. Using the bamboo mat, tightly roll the sushi away from you, pressing gently to seal the edge. Dampen the top edge of the nori with a little water to help it stick.
10. Repeat the process with the remaining nori sheets and ingredients.
11. Using a sharp knife dipped in water, slice each roll into 6-8 pieces.
12. Serve the Dragon Rolls with soy sauce, pickled ginger, and wasabi on the side. Optionally, sprinkle sesame seeds on top for garnish.

Enjoy your homemade Dragon Rolls!

Rainbow Roll

Ingredients:

- 2 cups sushi rice
- 2 1/2 cups water
- 1/2 cup rice vinegar
- 2 tablespoons sugar
- 1 teaspoon salt
- 4 sheets nori seaweed
- 8 ounces sushi-grade fish (such as tuna, salmon, yellowtail), thinly sliced
- 1 ripe avocado, thinly sliced
- 1/2 cucumber, peeled, seeded, and cut into matchsticks
- Crab sticks (optional)
- Soy sauce, for serving
- Pickled ginger, for serving
- Wasabi, for serving
- Sesame seeds, for garnish (optional)

Instructions:

1. Rinse the sushi rice under cold water until the water runs clear. Cook the rice either in a rice cooker or on the stovetop according to the package instructions. Let it cool to room temperature.
2. In a small saucepan, combine the rice vinegar, sugar, and salt. Heat over medium heat until the sugar and salt dissolve. Remove from heat and let the mixture cool.
3. Once the rice is cooled, gently fold in the vinegar mixture until well combined. Set aside.
4. Place a sheet of nori seaweed on a bamboo sushi mat, shiny side down. With wet hands, spread about 1/2 cup of sushi rice evenly over the nori, leaving a 1-inch border at the top edge.
5. Arrange slices of avocado and cucumber matchsticks across the center of the rice.
6. If using crab sticks, place them on top of the avocado and cucumber.
7. Carefully place slices of sushi-grade fish on top of the avocado, cucumber, and crab sticks, alternating colors to create a rainbow effect.
8. Using the bamboo mat, tightly roll the sushi away from you, pressing gently to seal the edge. Dampen the top edge of the nori with a little water to help it stick.

9. Repeat the process with the remaining nori sheets and ingredients.
10. Using a sharp knife dipped in water, slice each roll into 6-8 pieces.
11. Serve the Rainbow Rolls with soy sauce, pickled ginger, and wasabi on the side. Optionally, sprinkle sesame seeds on top for garnish.

Enjoy your homemade Rainbow Rolls!

Philadelphia Roll

Ingredients:

- 2 cups sushi rice
- 2 1/2 cups water
- 1/2 cup rice vinegar
- 2 tablespoons sugar
- 1 teaspoon salt
- 4 sheets nori seaweed
- 8 ounces sushi-grade salmon, thinly sliced
- 4 ounces cream cheese, softened
- 1 cucumber, peeled, seeded, and cut into matchsticks
- Soy sauce, for serving
- Pickled ginger, for serving
- Wasabi, for serving
- Sesame seeds, for garnish (optional)

Instructions:

1. Rinse the sushi rice under cold water until the water runs clear. Cook the rice either in a rice cooker or on the stovetop according to the package instructions. Let it cool to room temperature.
2. In a small saucepan, combine the rice vinegar, sugar, and salt. Heat over medium heat until the sugar and salt dissolve. Remove from heat and let the mixture cool.
3. Once the rice is cooled, gently fold in the vinegar mixture until well combined. Set aside.
4. Place a sheet of nori seaweed on a bamboo sushi mat, shiny side down. With wet hands, spread about 1/2 cup of sushi rice evenly over the nori, leaving a 1-inch border at the top edge.
5. Spread a thin layer of softened cream cheese across the center of the rice.
6. Arrange slices of sushi-grade salmon and cucumber matchsticks on top of the cream cheese.
7. Using the bamboo mat, tightly roll the sushi away from you, pressing gently to seal the edge. Dampen the top edge of the nori with a little water to help it stick.
8. Repeat the process with the remaining nori sheets and ingredients.
9. Using a sharp knife dipped in water, slice each roll into 6-8 pieces.
10. Serve the Philadelphia Rolls with soy sauce, pickled ginger, and wasabi on the side. Optionally, sprinkle sesame seeds on top for garnish.

Enjoy your homemade Philadelphia Rolls!

Salmon Avocado Roll

Ingredients:

- 2 cups sushi rice
- 2 1/2 cups water
- 1/2 cup rice vinegar
- 2 tablespoons sugar
- 1 teaspoon salt
- 4 sheets nori seaweed
- 8 ounces sushi-grade salmon, thinly sliced
- 1 ripe avocado, thinly sliced
- Soy sauce, for serving
- Pickled ginger, for serving
- Wasabi, for serving
- Sesame seeds, for garnish (optional)

Instructions:

1. Rinse the sushi rice under cold water until the water runs clear. Cook the rice either in a rice cooker or on the stovetop according to the package instructions. Let it cool to room temperature.
2. In a small saucepan, combine the rice vinegar, sugar, and salt. Heat over medium heat until the sugar and salt dissolve. Remove from heat and let the mixture cool.
3. Once the rice is cooled, gently fold in the vinegar mixture until well combined. Set aside.
4. Place a sheet of nori seaweed on a bamboo sushi mat, shiny side down. With wet hands, spread about 1/2 cup of sushi rice evenly over the nori, leaving a 1-inch border at the top edge.
5. Arrange slices of sushi-grade salmon and avocado across the center of the rice.
6. Using the bamboo mat, tightly roll the sushi away from you, pressing gently to seal the edge. Dampen the top edge of the nori with a little water to help it stick.
7. Repeat the process with the remaining nori sheets and ingredients.
8. Using a sharp knife dipped in water, slice each roll into 6-8 pieces.
9. Serve the Salmon Avocado Rolls with soy sauce, pickled ginger, and wasabi on the side. Optionally, sprinkle sesame seeds on top for garnish.

Enjoy your homemade Salmon Avocado Rolls!

Dynamite Roll

Ingredients:

- 2 cups sushi rice
- 2 1/2 cups water
- 1/2 cup rice vinegar
- 2 tablespoons sugar
- 1 teaspoon salt
- 4 sheets nori seaweed
- 8 ounces cooked shrimp, peeled and deveined
- 1/2 cup mayonnaise
- 1 tablespoon Sriracha sauce (adjust to taste)
- 1 teaspoon sesame oil
- 1/2 cucumber, peeled, seeded, and cut into matchsticks
- Soy sauce, for serving
- Pickled ginger, for serving
- Wasabi, for serving
- Sesame seeds, for garnish (optional)

Instructions:

1. Rinse the sushi rice under cold water until the water runs clear. Cook the rice either in a rice cooker or on the stovetop according to the package instructions. Let it cool to room temperature.
2. In a small saucepan, combine the rice vinegar, sugar, and salt. Heat over medium heat until the sugar and salt dissolve. Remove from heat and let the mixture cool.
3. Once the rice is cooled, gently fold in the vinegar mixture until well combined. Set aside.
4. In a bowl, mix together the mayonnaise, Sriracha sauce, and sesame oil until smooth.
5. Chop the cooked shrimp into small pieces and mix them with the spicy mayonnaise mixture.
6. Place a sheet of nori seaweed on a bamboo sushi mat, shiny side down. With wet hands, spread about 1/2 cup of sushi rice evenly over the nori, leaving a 1-inch border at the top edge.
7. Spread a thin layer of the shrimp and mayonnaise mixture across the center of the rice.

8. Arrange cucumber matchsticks on top of the shrimp mixture.
9. Using the bamboo mat, tightly roll the sushi away from you, pressing gently to seal the edge. Dampen the top edge of the nori with a little water to help it stick.
10. Repeat the process with the remaining nori sheets and ingredients.
11. Using a sharp knife dipped in water, slice each roll into 6-8 pieces.
12. Serve the Dynamite Rolls with soy sauce, pickled ginger, and wasabi on the side. Optionally, sprinkle sesame seeds on top for garnish.

Enjoy your homemade Dynamite Rolls!

Spider Roll

Ingredients:

- 2 cups sushi rice
- 2 1/2 cups water
- 1/2 cup rice vinegar
- 2 tablespoons sugar
- 1 teaspoon salt
- 4 sheets nori seaweed
- 8 ounces soft shell crab (cleaned and prepared)
- 1/2 cup all-purpose flour
- 1/2 cup cornstarch
- 1 teaspoon salt
- Vegetable oil for frying
- 1 ripe avocado, thinly sliced
- 1/2 cucumber, peeled, seeded, and cut into matchsticks
- Soy sauce, for serving
- Pickled ginger, for serving
- Wasabi, for serving
- Sesame seeds, for garnish (optional)

Instructions:

1. Rinse the sushi rice under cold water until the water runs clear. Cook the rice either in a rice cooker or on the stovetop according to the package instructions. Let it cool to room temperature.
2. In a small saucepan, combine the rice vinegar, sugar, and salt. Heat over medium heat until the sugar and salt dissolve. Remove from heat and let the mixture cool.
3. Once the rice is cooled, gently fold in the vinegar mixture until well combined. Set aside.
4. In a shallow bowl, mix together the all-purpose flour, cornstarch, and salt.
5. Dredge the soft shell crab in the flour mixture, shaking off any excess.
6. Heat vegetable oil in a deep fryer or large skillet to 350°F (175°C). Carefully fry the soft shell crab until golden brown and crispy, about 3-4 minutes. Remove from oil and drain on paper towels.

7. Place a sheet of nori seaweed on a bamboo sushi mat, shiny side down. With wet hands, spread about 1/2 cup of sushi rice evenly over the nori, leaving a 1-inch border at the top edge.
8. Arrange slices of avocado and cucumber matchsticks across the center of the rice.
9. Place the fried soft shell crab on top of the avocado and cucumber.
10. Using the bamboo mat, tightly roll the sushi away from you, pressing gently to seal the edge. Dampen the top edge of the nori with a little water to help it stick.
11. Repeat the process with the remaining nori sheets and ingredients.
12. Using a sharp knife dipped in water, slice each roll into 6-8 pieces.
13. Serve the Spider Rolls with soy sauce, pickled ginger, and wasabi on the side. Optionally, sprinkle sesame seeds on top for garnish.

Enjoy your homemade Spider Rolls!

Tempura Shrimp Roll

Ingredients:

- 2 cups sushi rice
- 2 1/2 cups water
- 1/2 cup rice vinegar
- 2 tablespoons sugar
- 1 teaspoon salt
- 4 sheets nori seaweed
- 8 large shrimp, peeled and deveined
- 1/2 cup all-purpose flour
- 1/2 cup cornstarch
- 1 teaspoon baking powder
- 1 cup ice water
- Vegetable oil for frying
- 1 ripe avocado, thinly sliced
- 1/2 cucumber, peeled, seeded, and cut into matchsticks
- Soy sauce, for serving
- Pickled ginger, for serving
- Wasabi, for serving
- Sesame seeds, for garnish (optional)

Instructions:

1. Rinse the sushi rice under cold water until the water runs clear. Cook the rice either in a rice cooker or on the stovetop according to the package instructions. Let it cool to room temperature.
2. In a small saucepan, combine the rice vinegar, sugar, and salt. Heat over medium heat until the sugar and salt dissolve. Remove from heat and let the mixture cool.
3. Once the rice is cooled, gently fold in the vinegar mixture until well combined. Set aside.
4. In a bowl, mix together the all-purpose flour, cornstarch, and baking powder. Gradually whisk in the ice water until the batter is smooth.
5. Heat vegetable oil in a deep fryer or large skillet to 350°F (175°C).
6. Dip each shrimp into the tempura batter, coating evenly. Carefully lower the shrimp into the hot oil and fry until golden brown and crispy, about 2-3 minutes. Remove from oil and drain on paper towels.

7. Place a sheet of nori seaweed on a bamboo sushi mat, shiny side down. With wet hands, spread about 1/2 cup of sushi rice evenly over the nori, leaving a 1-inch border at the top edge.
8. Arrange slices of avocado and cucumber matchsticks across the center of the rice.
9. Place the tempura shrimp on top of the avocado and cucumber.
10. Using the bamboo mat, tightly roll the sushi away from you, pressing gently to seal the edge. Dampen the top edge of the nori with a little water to help it stick.
11. Repeat the process with the remaining nori sheets and ingredients.
12. Using a sharp knife dipped in water, slice each roll into 6-8 pieces.
13. Serve the Tempura Shrimp Rolls with soy sauce, pickled ginger, and wasabi on the side. Optionally, sprinkle sesame seeds on top for garnish.

Enjoy your homemade Tempura Shrimp Rolls!

Caterpillar Roll

Ingredients:

- 2 cups sushi rice
- 2 1/2 cups water
- 1/2 cup rice vinegar
- 2 tablespoons sugar
- 1 teaspoon salt
- 4 sheets nori seaweed
- 8 ounces sushi-grade eel (unagi), sliced
- 1 ripe avocado, thinly sliced
- Soy sauce, for serving
- Pickled ginger, for serving
- Wasabi, for serving
- Sesame seeds, for garnish (optional)
- Eel sauce (store-bought or homemade) for drizzling

Instructions:

1. Rinse the sushi rice under cold water until the water runs clear. Cook the rice either in a rice cooker or on the stovetop according to the package instructions. Let it cool to room temperature.
2. In a small saucepan, combine the rice vinegar, sugar, and salt. Heat over medium heat until the sugar and salt dissolve. Remove from heat and let the mixture cool.
3. Once the rice is cooled, gently fold in the vinegar mixture until well combined. Set aside.
4. Place a sheet of nori seaweed on a bamboo sushi mat, shiny side down. With wet hands, spread about 1/2 cup of sushi rice evenly over the nori, leaving a 1-inch border at the top edge.
5. Arrange slices of avocado across the center of the rice.
6. Place slices of sushi-grade eel on top of the avocado, slightly overlapping them.
7. Using the bamboo mat, tightly roll the sushi away from you, pressing gently to seal the edge. Dampen the top edge of the nori with a little water to help it stick.
8. Place the roll seam-side down on a cutting board. Using a sharp knife dipped in water, cut off about 1/4 inch from both ends of the roll to make them neat.
9. Cut the remaining roll into 8 equal pieces.
10. Arrange the pieces on a serving plate, curving them slightly to resemble a caterpillar.

11. Drizzle eel sauce over the top of the roll to create the "caterpillar" effect.
12. Serve the Caterpillar Roll with soy sauce, pickled ginger, and wasabi on the side. Optionally, sprinkle sesame seeds on top for garnish.

Enjoy your homemade Caterpillar Roll!

Veggie Roll

Ingredients:

- 2 cups sushi rice
- 2 1/2 cups water
- 1/2 cup rice vinegar
- 2 tablespoons sugar
- 1 teaspoon salt
- 4 sheets nori seaweed
- 1/2 cucumber, peeled, seeded, and cut into matchsticks
- 1 avocado, thinly sliced
- 1 carrot, peeled and cut into matchsticks
- 1/2 red bell pepper, thinly sliced
- 1/2 yellow bell pepper, thinly sliced
- Soy sauce, for serving
- Pickled ginger, for serving
- Wasabi, for serving

Instructions:

1. Rinse the sushi rice under cold water until the water runs clear. Cook the rice either in a rice cooker or on the stovetop according to the package instructions. Let it cool to room temperature.
2. In a small saucepan, combine the rice vinegar, sugar, and salt. Heat over medium heat until the sugar and salt dissolve. Remove from heat and let the mixture cool.
3. Once the rice is cooled, gently fold in the vinegar mixture until well combined. Set aside.
4. Place a sheet of nori seaweed on a bamboo sushi mat, shiny side down. With wet hands, spread about 1/2 cup of sushi rice evenly over the nori, leaving a 1-inch border at the top edge.
5. Arrange cucumber, avocado, carrot, and bell pepper strips across the center of the rice.
6. Using the bamboo mat, tightly roll the sushi away from you, pressing gently to seal the edge. Dampen the top edge of the nori with a little water to help it stick.
7. Repeat the process with the remaining nori sheets and ingredients.
8. Using a sharp knife dipped in water, slice each roll into 6-8 pieces.
9. Serve the Veggie Rolls with soy sauce, pickled ginger, and wasabi on the side.

Enjoy your homemade Veggie Rolls!

Dragonfly Roll

Ingredients:

- 4 sheets of nori (seaweed)
- 2 cups sushi rice, cooked
- 8 shrimp tempura, cooked
- 1/2 cucumber, julienned
- 1 ripe avocado, thinly sliced
- Spicy mayo (store-bought or homemade)
- Eel sauce (store-bought or homemade)
- Soy sauce, for dipping (optional)
- Pickled ginger, for serving (optional)
- Wasabi, for serving (optional)
- Sesame seeds, for garnish (optional)

Instructions:

1. Lay a sheet of nori on a bamboo sushi rolling mat (makisu), shiny side down.
2. With wet hands, spread a thin layer of sushi rice evenly over the nori, leaving about a 1-inch border along the top edge.
3. Place 2 shrimp tempura, cucumber strips, and avocado slices in a line across the middle of the rice-covered nori sheet.
4. Using the bamboo mat, tightly roll the nori sheet around the filling ingredients, pressing gently to seal the edge. Roll until you reach the top edge of the nori.
5. Using a sharp knife, slice the rolled sushi into 8 equal pieces.
6. Arrange the sliced pieces on a serving plate.
7. Drizzle the Dragonfly Roll with spicy mayo and eel sauce.
8. Optionally, sprinkle sesame seeds over the top for garnish.
9. Serve the Dragonfly Roll with soy sauce, pickled ginger, and wasabi on the side, if desired.
10. Enjoy your homemade Dragonfly Roll as a delicious and satisfying sushi treat!

Feel free to customize the Dragonfly Roll with additional fillings or toppings according to your taste preferences. You can also adjust the spiciness of the mayo and the sweetness of the eel sauce to suit your liking.

Crunchy Roll

Ingredients:

- 2 cups sushi rice
- 2 1/2 cups water
- 1/2 cup rice vinegar
- 2 tablespoons sugar
- 1 teaspoon salt
- 4 sheets nori seaweed
- 8 ounces sushi-grade fish (such as tuna or salmon), thinly sliced
- 1/2 cucumber, peeled, seeded, and cut into matchsticks
- 1 avocado, thinly sliced
- 1/4 cup mayonnaise
- 1 tablespoon Sriracha sauce (adjust to taste)
- 1 cup tempura flakes
- Soy sauce, for serving
- Pickled ginger, for serving
- Wasabi, for serving

Instructions:

1. Rinse the sushi rice under cold water until the water runs clear. Cook the rice either in a rice cooker or on the stovetop according to the package instructions. Let it cool to room temperature.
2. In a small saucepan, combine the rice vinegar, sugar, and salt. Heat over medium heat until the sugar and salt dissolve. Remove from heat and let the mixture cool.
3. Once the rice is cooled, gently fold in the vinegar mixture until well combined. Set aside.
4. Place a sheet of nori seaweed on a bamboo sushi mat, shiny side down. With wet hands, spread about 1/2 cup of sushi rice evenly over the nori, leaving a 1-inch border at the top edge.
5. Arrange slices of sushi-grade fish, cucumber matchsticks, and avocado across the center of the rice.
6. In a small bowl, mix together the mayonnaise and Sriracha sauce until well combined. Spread a thin layer of the spicy mayonnaise mixture over the ingredients on the rice.
7. Sprinkle tempura flakes evenly over the spicy mayonnaise layer.

8. Using the bamboo mat, tightly roll the sushi away from you, pressing gently to seal the edge. Dampen the top edge of the nori with a little water to help it stick.
9. Repeat the process with the remaining nori sheets and ingredients.
10. Using a sharp knife dipped in water, slice each roll into 6-8 pieces.
11. Serve the Crunchy Rolls with soy sauce, pickled ginger, and wasabi on the side.

Enjoy your homemade Crunchy Rolls!

Lobster Roll

Ingredients:

- 2 lobster tails (about 8 ounces each)
- 2 tablespoons butter, melted
- Salt and pepper to taste
- 2 cups sushi rice
- 2 1/2 cups water
- 1/2 cup rice vinegar
- 2 tablespoons sugar
- 1 teaspoon salt
- 4 sheets nori seaweed
- 1 avocado, thinly sliced
- 1/2 cucumber, peeled, seeded, and cut into matchsticks
- Soy sauce, for serving
- Pickled ginger, for serving
- Wasabi, for serving
- Optional: mayonnaise or spicy mayo for drizzling

Instructions:

1. Preheat the oven to 375°F (190°C).
2. Prepare the lobster tails by cutting the top shell lengthwise, exposing the meat. Brush the meat with melted butter and season with salt and pepper.
3. Place the lobster tails on a baking sheet and roast in the preheated oven for about 12-15 minutes, or until the meat is opaque and cooked through. Remove from the oven and let them cool slightly.
4. Once the lobster tails are cool enough to handle, remove the meat from the shells and chop it into bite-sized pieces.
5. Rinse the sushi rice under cold water until the water runs clear. Cook the rice either in a rice cooker or on the stovetop according to the package instructions. Let it cool to room temperature.
6. In a small saucepan, combine the rice vinegar, sugar, and salt. Heat over medium heat until the sugar and salt dissolve. Remove from heat and let the mixture cool.
7. Once the rice is cooled, gently fold in the vinegar mixture until well combined. Set aside.

8. Place a sheet of nori seaweed on a bamboo sushi mat, shiny side down. With wet hands, spread about 1/2 cup of sushi rice evenly over the nori, leaving a 1-inch border at the top edge.
9. Arrange slices of avocado and cucumber matchsticks across the center of the rice.
10. Add the chopped lobster meat on top of the avocado and cucumber.
11. Optionally, drizzle some mayonnaise or spicy mayo over the lobster meat.
12. Using the bamboo mat, tightly roll the sushi away from you, pressing gently to seal the edge. Dampen the top edge of the nori with a little water to help it stick.
13. Repeat the process with the remaining nori sheets and ingredients.
14. Using a sharp knife dipped in water, slice each roll into 6-8 pieces.

Serve the Lobster Rolls with soy sauce, pickled ginger, and wasabi on the side.

15. Enjoy your homemade Lobster Rolls!

Teriyaki Chicken Roll

Ingredients:

- 2 boneless, skinless chicken breasts
- 1/2 cup teriyaki sauce (store-bought or homemade)
- 2 cups sushi rice
- 2 1/2 cups water
- 1/2 cup rice vinegar
- 2 tablespoons sugar
- 1 teaspoon salt
- 4 sheets nori seaweed
- 1/2 cucumber, peeled, seeded, and cut into matchsticks
- Soy sauce, for serving
- Pickled ginger, for serving
- Wasabi, for serving
- Sesame seeds, for garnish (optional)

Instructions:

1. Preheat the oven to 375°F (190°C).
2. Place the chicken breasts in a baking dish and pour the teriyaki sauce over them, ensuring they are well coated. Marinate for at least 30 minutes.
3. Bake the chicken in the preheated oven for about 20-25 minutes, or until cooked through. Remove from the oven and let it cool. Once cooled, slice the chicken into thin strips.
4. Rinse the sushi rice under cold water until the water runs clear. Cook the rice either in a rice cooker or on the stovetop according to the package instructions. Let it cool to room temperature.
5. In a small saucepan, combine the rice vinegar, sugar, and salt. Heat over medium heat until the sugar and salt dissolve. Remove from heat and let the mixture cool.
6. Once the rice is cooled, gently fold in the vinegar mixture until well combined. Set aside.
7. Place a sheet of nori seaweed on a bamboo sushi mat, shiny side down. With wet hands, spread about 1/2 cup of sushi rice evenly over the nori, leaving a 1-inch border at the top edge.
8. Arrange slices of cucumber and teriyaki chicken strips across the center of the rice.

9. Using the bamboo mat, tightly roll the sushi away from you, pressing gently to seal the edge. Dampen the top edge of the nori with a little water to help it stick.
10. Repeat the process with the remaining nori sheets and ingredients.
11. Using a sharp knife dipped in water, slice each roll into 6-8 pieces.

Serve the Teriyaki Chicken Rolls with soy sauce, pickled ginger, and wasabi on the side. Optionally, sprinkle sesame seeds on top for garnish.

12. Enjoy your homemade Teriyaki Chicken Rolls!

Scallop Roll

Ingredients:

- 1 cup sushi rice
- 1 1/4 cups water
- 2 tablespoons rice vinegar
- 1 tablespoon sugar
- 1/2 teaspoon salt
- 4 large scallops, fresh or thawed
- Salt and pepper, to taste
- 1 tablespoon vegetable oil
- 1/2 cucumber, peeled, seeded, and cut into matchsticks
- 1 avocado, thinly sliced
- 4 sheets nori seaweed
- Soy sauce, for serving
- Pickled ginger, for serving
- Wasabi, for serving
- Sesame seeds, for garnish (optional)

Instructions:

1. Rinse the sushi rice under cold water until the water runs clear. Combine the rinsed rice and water in a rice cooker and cook according to the manufacturer's instructions. Alternatively, cook the rice in a pot on the stovetop. Once cooked, let the rice cool slightly.
2. In a small saucepan, combine the rice vinegar, sugar, and salt. Heat over low heat until the sugar and salt dissolve. Remove from heat and let it cool.
3. Spread the cooked rice onto a large plate or shallow dish. Drizzle the seasoned rice vinegar over the rice and gently fold it in using a spatula or rice paddle. Allow the rice to cool completely to room temperature.
4. Pat the scallops dry with paper towels and season them with salt and pepper on both sides.
5. Heat the vegetable oil in a skillet over medium-high heat. Once hot, add the scallops and sear them for 1-2 minutes on each side, or until golden brown and cooked through. Remove from heat and let them cool slightly.
6. Once the scallops are cool enough to handle, slice them thinly.

7. Place a sheet of nori seaweed on a bamboo sushi mat, shiny side down. With wet hands, spread an even layer of sushi rice over the nori, leaving a small border along the top edge.
8. Arrange slices of cucumber, avocado, and scallops across the center of the rice.
9. Using the bamboo mat, tightly roll the sushi away from you, pressing gently to seal the edge. Dampen the top edge of the nori with a little water to help it stick.
10. Repeat the process with the remaining nori sheets and ingredients.
11. Using a sharp knife dipped in water, slice each roll into 6-8 pieces.
12. Serve the Scallop Rolls with soy sauce, pickled ginger, and wasabi on the side. Optionally, sprinkle sesame seeds on top for garnish.

Enjoy your homemade Scallop Rolls!

Volcano Roll

Ingredients:

- 2 cups sushi rice
- 2 1/2 cups water
- 1/2 cup rice vinegar
- 2 tablespoons sugar
- 1 teaspoon salt
- 4 sheets nori seaweed
- 8 ounces sushi-grade fish (such as tuna or salmon), thinly sliced
- 1/2 cucumber, peeled, seeded, and cut into matchsticks
- 1 avocado, thinly sliced
- 4 imitation crab sticks, shredded
- 1/4 cup mayonnaise
- 1 tablespoon Sriracha sauce (adjust to taste)
- 1 tablespoon masago (fish roe), for garnish
- Soy sauce, for serving
- Pickled ginger, for serving
- Wasabi, for serving

Instructions:

1. Rinse the sushi rice under cold water until the water runs clear. Cook the rice either in a rice cooker or on the stovetop according to the package instructions. Let it cool to room temperature.
2. In a small saucepan, combine the rice vinegar, sugar, and salt. Heat over medium heat until the sugar and salt dissolve. Remove from heat and let the mixture cool.
3. Once the rice is cooled, gently fold in the vinegar mixture until well combined. Set aside.
4. Place a sheet of nori seaweed on a bamboo sushi mat, shiny side down. With wet hands, spread about 1/2 cup of sushi rice evenly over the nori, leaving a 1-inch border at the top edge.
5. Arrange slices of sushi-grade fish, cucumber matchsticks, avocado slices, and shredded imitation crab sticks across the center of the rice.
6. In a small bowl, mix together the mayonnaise and Sriracha sauce until well combined. Drizzle the spicy mayonnaise mixture over the ingredients on the rice.

7. Roll the sushi tightly away from you using the bamboo mat, pressing gently to seal the edge. Dampen the top edge of the nori with a little water to help it stick.
8. Place the roll on a serving plate and shape it into a volcano-like mound.
9. Use a blowtorch to lightly torch the top of the roll to create a charred effect.
10. Sprinkle masago (fish roe) over the top of the roll for garnish.
11. Serve the Volcano Roll with soy sauce, pickled ginger, and wasabi on the side.

Enjoy your homemade Volcano Roll!

Mango Tango Roll

Ingredients:

- 2 cups sushi rice
- 2 1/2 cups water
- 1/2 cup rice vinegar
- 2 tablespoons sugar
- 1 teaspoon salt
- 4 sheets nori seaweed
- 8 ounces sushi-grade fish (such as tuna or salmon), thinly sliced
- 1 ripe mango, peeled and thinly sliced
- 1/2 cucumber, peeled, seeded, and cut into matchsticks
- 4 imitation crab sticks, shredded
- Soy sauce, for serving
- Pickled ginger, for serving
- Wasabi, for serving

Instructions:

1. Rinse the sushi rice under cold water until the water runs clear. Cook the rice either in a rice cooker or on the stovetop according to the package instructions. Let it cool to room temperature.
2. In a small saucepan, combine the rice vinegar, sugar, and salt. Heat over medium heat until the sugar and salt dissolve. Remove from heat and let the mixture cool.
3. Once the rice is cooled, gently fold in the vinegar mixture until well combined. Set aside.
4. Place a sheet of nori seaweed on a bamboo sushi mat, shiny side down. With wet hands, spread about 1/2 cup of sushi rice evenly over the nori, leaving a 1-inch border at the top edge.
5. Arrange slices of sushi-grade fish, mango slices, cucumber matchsticks, and shredded imitation crab sticks across the center of the rice.
6. Roll the sushi tightly away from you using the bamboo mat, pressing gently to seal the edge. Dampen the top edge of the nori with a little water to help it stick.
7. Repeat the process with the remaining nori sheets and ingredients.
8. Using a sharp knife dipped in water, slice each roll into 6-8 pieces.
9. Serve the Mango Tango Roll with soy sauce, pickled ginger, and wasabi on the side.

Enjoy your homemade Mango Tango Roll!

Hawaiian Roll

Ingredients:

- 2 cups sushi rice
- 2 1/2 cups water
- 1/2 cup rice vinegar
- 2 tablespoons sugar
- 1 teaspoon salt
- 4 sheets nori seaweed
- 8 ounces sushi-grade tuna, thinly sliced
- 1/2 ripe mango, thinly sliced
- 1/2 avocado, thinly sliced
- 1/4 cup sliced pineapple
- Soy sauce, for serving
- Pickled ginger, for serving
- Wasabi, for serving

Instructions:

1. Rinse the sushi rice under cold water until the water runs clear. Cook the rice either in a rice cooker or on the stovetop according to the package instructions. Let it cool to room temperature.
2. In a small saucepan, combine the rice vinegar, sugar, and salt. Heat over medium heat until the sugar and salt dissolve. Remove from heat and let the mixture cool.
3. Once the rice is cooled, gently fold in the vinegar mixture until well combined. Set aside.
4. Place a sheet of nori seaweed on a bamboo sushi mat, shiny side down. With wet hands, spread about 1/2 cup of sushi rice evenly over the nori, leaving a 1-inch border at the top edge.
5. Arrange slices of sushi-grade tuna, mango, avocado, and pineapple across the center of the rice.
6. Roll the sushi tightly away from you using the bamboo mat, pressing gently to seal the edge. Dampen the top edge of the nori with a little water to help it stick.
7. Repeat the process with the remaining nori sheets and ingredients.
8. Using a sharp knife dipped in water, slice each roll into 6-8 pieces.
9. Serve the Hawaiian Roll with soy sauce, pickled ginger, and wasabi on the side.

Enjoy your homemade Hawaiian Roll!

Cucumber Roll

Ingredients:

- 2 cups sushi rice
- 2 1/2 cups water
- 1/2 cup rice vinegar
- 2 tablespoons sugar
- 1 teaspoon salt
- 4 sheets nori seaweed
- 1 large cucumber, peeled and cut into long thin strips
- Soy sauce, for serving
- Pickled ginger, for serving
- Wasabi, for serving

Instructions:

1. Rinse the sushi rice under cold water until the water runs clear. Cook the rice either in a rice cooker or on the stovetop according to the package instructions. Let it cool to room temperature.
2. In a small saucepan, combine the rice vinegar, sugar, and salt. Heat over medium heat until the sugar and salt dissolve. Remove from heat and let the mixture cool.
3. Once the rice is cooled, gently fold in the vinegar mixture until well combined. Set aside.
4. Place a sheet of nori seaweed on a bamboo sushi mat, shiny side down. With wet hands, spread about 1/2 cup of sushi rice evenly over the nori, leaving a 1-inch border at the top edge.
5. Arrange strips of cucumber across the center of the rice.
6. Roll the sushi tightly away from you using the bamboo mat, pressing gently to seal the edge. Dampen the top edge of the nori with a little water to help it stick.
7. Repeat the process with the remaining nori sheets and ingredients.
8. Using a sharp knife dipped in water, slice each roll into 6-8 pieces.
9. Serve the Cucumber Rolls with soy sauce, pickled ginger, and wasabi on the side.

Enjoy your homemade Cucumber Rolls!

Philadelphia Crunch Roll

Ingredients:

- 2 cups sushi rice
- 2 1/2 cups water
- 1/2 cup rice vinegar
- 2 tablespoons sugar
- 1 teaspoon salt
- 4 sheets nori seaweed
- 8 ounces sushi-grade salmon, thinly sliced
- 4 ounces cream cheese, softened
- 1/2 cucumber, peeled, seeded, and cut into matchsticks
- 1/4 cup tempura flakes
- Soy sauce, for serving
- Pickled ginger, for serving
- Wasabi, for serving

Instructions:

1. Rinse the sushi rice under cold water until the water runs clear. Cook the rice either in a rice cooker or on the stovetop according to the package instructions. Let it cool to room temperature.
2. In a small saucepan, combine the rice vinegar, sugar, and salt. Heat over medium heat until the sugar and salt dissolve. Remove from heat and let the mixture cool.
3. Once the rice is cooled, gently fold in the vinegar mixture until well combined. Set aside.
4. Place a sheet of nori seaweed on a bamboo sushi mat, shiny side down. With wet hands, spread about 1/2 cup of sushi rice evenly over the nori, leaving a 1-inch border at the top edge.
5. Spread a thin layer of cream cheese over the rice.
6. Arrange slices of sushi-grade salmon and cucumber matchsticks across the center of the rice.
7. Sprinkle tempura flakes evenly over the salmon and cucumber.
8. Roll the sushi tightly away from you using the bamboo mat, pressing gently to seal the edge. Dampen the top edge of the nori with a little water to help it stick.
9. Repeat the process with the remaining nori sheets and ingredients.
10. Using a sharp knife dipped in water, slice each roll into 6-8 pieces.

11. Serve the Philadelphia Crunch Rolls with soy sauce, pickled ginger, and wasabi on the side.

Enjoy your homemade Philadelphia Crunch Rolls!

Soft Shell Crab Roll

Ingredients:

- 2 soft shell crabs, cleaned
- 1 cup all-purpose flour
- 1 teaspoon salt
- 1/2 teaspoon black pepper
- Vegetable oil for frying
- 2 cups sushi rice
- 2 1/2 cups water
- 1/2 cup rice vinegar
- 2 tablespoons sugar
- 1 teaspoon salt
- 4 sheets nori seaweed
- 1/2 cucumber, peeled, seeded, and cut into matchsticks
- Soy sauce, for serving
- Pickled ginger, for serving
- Wasabi, for serving

Instructions:

1. Rinse the soft shell crabs under cold water and pat them dry with paper towels.
2. In a shallow dish, combine the all-purpose flour, salt, and black pepper.
3. Heat vegetable oil in a large skillet or deep fryer to 350°F (175°C).
4. Dredge each soft shell crab in the flour mixture, shaking off any excess.
5. Carefully place the crabs in the hot oil and fry for about 2-3 minutes on each side, or until they are golden brown and crispy. Remove from the oil and drain on paper towels.
6. Rinse the sushi rice under cold water until the water runs clear. Cook the rice either in a rice cooker or on the stovetop according to the package instructions. Let it cool to room temperature.
7. In a small saucepan, combine the rice vinegar, sugar, and salt. Heat over medium heat until the sugar and salt dissolve. Remove from heat and let the mixture cool.
8. Once the rice is cooled, gently fold in the vinegar mixture until well combined. Set aside.

9. Place a sheet of nori seaweed on a bamboo sushi mat, shiny side down. With wet hands, spread about 1/2 cup of sushi rice evenly over the nori, leaving a 1-inch border at the top edge.
10. Arrange strips of cucumber across the center of the rice.
11. Place one soft shell crab on top of the cucumber.
12. Roll the sushi tightly away from you using the bamboo mat, pressing gently to seal the edge. Dampen the top edge of the nori with a little water to help it stick.
13. Repeat the process with the remaining nori sheets and ingredients.
14. Using a sharp knife dipped in water, slice each roll into 6-8 pieces.
15. Serve the Soft Shell Crab Rolls with soy sauce, pickled ginger, and wasabi on the side.

Enjoy your homemade Soft Shell Crab Rolls!

Shrimp Tempura Roll

Ingredients:

- 8 large shrimp, peeled and deveined
- 1 cup all-purpose flour
- 1 teaspoon salt
- 1/2 teaspoon black pepper
- 1 cup cold water
- Vegetable oil for frying
- 2 cups sushi rice
- 2 1/2 cups water
- 1/2 cup rice vinegar
- 2 tablespoons sugar
- 1 teaspoon salt
- 4 sheets nori seaweed
- 1/2 cucumber, peeled, seeded, and cut into matchsticks
- Soy sauce, for serving
- Pickled ginger, for serving
- Wasabi, for serving

Instructions:

1. Rinse the sushi rice under cold water until the water runs clear. Cook the rice either in a rice cooker or on the stovetop according to the package instructions. Let it cool to room temperature.
2. In a small saucepan, combine the rice vinegar, sugar, and salt. Heat over medium heat until the sugar and salt dissolve. Remove from heat and let the mixture cool.
3. Once the rice is cooled, gently fold in the vinegar mixture until well combined. Set aside.
4. In a large bowl, whisk together the all-purpose flour, salt, pepper, and cold water until smooth.
5. Heat vegetable oil in a large skillet or deep fryer to 350°F (175°C).
6. Dip each shrimp into the tempura batter, coating evenly. Carefully lower the shrimp into the hot oil and fry until golden brown and crispy, about 2-3 minutes. Remove from oil and drain on paper towels.

7. Place a sheet of nori seaweed on a bamboo sushi mat, shiny side down. With wet hands, spread about 1/2 cup of sushi rice evenly over the nori, leaving a 1-inch border at the top edge.
8. Arrange strips of cucumber across the center of the rice.
9. Place two shrimp tempura on top of the cucumber.
10. Roll the sushi tightly away from you using the bamboo mat, pressing gently to seal the edge. Dampen the top edge of the nori with a little water to help it stick.
11. Repeat the process with the remaining nori sheets and ingredients.
12. Using a sharp knife dipped in water, slice each roll into 6-8 pieces.
13. Serve the Shrimp Tempura Rolls with soy sauce, pickled ginger, and wasabi on the side.

Enjoy your homemade Shrimp Tempura Rolls!

Unagi Roll

Ingredients:

- 8 large shrimp, peeled and deveined
- 1 cup all-purpose flour
- 1 teaspoon salt
- 1/2 teaspoon black pepper
- 1 cup cold water
- Vegetable oil for frying
- 2 cups sushi rice
- 2 1/2 cups water
- 1/2 cup rice vinegar
- 2 tablespoons sugar
- 1 teaspoon salt
- 4 sheets nori seaweed
- 1/2 cucumber, peeled, seeded, and cut into matchsticks
- Soy sauce, for serving
- Pickled ginger, for serving
- Wasabi, for serving

Instructions:

1. Rinse the sushi rice under cold water until the water runs clear. Cook the rice either in a rice cooker or on the stovetop according to the package instructions. Let it cool to room temperature.
2. In a small saucepan, combine the rice vinegar, sugar, and salt. Heat over medium heat until the sugar and salt dissolve. Remove from heat and let the mixture cool.
3. Once the rice is cooled, gently fold in the vinegar mixture until well combined. Set aside.
4. In a large bowl, whisk together the all-purpose flour, salt, pepper, and cold water until smooth.
5. Heat vegetable oil in a large skillet or deep fryer to 350°F (175°C).
6. Dip each shrimp into the tempura batter, coating evenly. Carefully lower the shrimp into the hot oil and fry until golden brown and crispy, about 2-3 minutes. Remove from oil and drain on paper towels.

7. Place a sheet of nori seaweed on a bamboo sushi mat, shiny side down. With wet hands, spread about 1/2 cup of sushi rice evenly over the nori, leaving a 1-inch border at the top edge.
8. Arrange strips of cucumber across the center of the rice.
9. Place two shrimp tempura on top of the cucumber.
10. Roll the sushi tightly away from you using the bamboo mat, pressing gently to seal the edge. Dampen the top edge of the nori with a little water to help it stick.
11. Repeat the process with the remaining nori sheets and ingredients.
12. Using a sharp knife dipped in water, slice each roll into 6-8 pieces.
13. Serve the Shrimp Tempura Rolls with soy sauce, pickled ginger, and wasabi on the side.

Enjoy your homemade Shrimp Tempura Rolls!

Tuna Nigiri

Ingredients:

- Sushi-grade tuna
- Sushi rice (prepared with rice vinegar, sugar, and salt)
- Soy sauce, for serving
- Wasabi, for serving
- Pickled ginger, for serving

Instructions:

1. Begin by preparing sushi rice according to package instructions. Once cooked, let it cool slightly before shaping into nigiri.
2. Cut the sushi-grade tuna into rectangular slices, about 1/4 inch thick and 1 inch wide. Make sure to use a sharp knife to ensure clean cuts.
3. With wet hands, take a small amount of sushi rice and shape it into an oval or rectangular mound, about 1 inch in length and 1/2 inch in width.
4. Place a slice of tuna over the top of the rice mound, gently pressing down to adhere the tuna to the rice.
5. Repeat the process to make more nigiri, using up all the tuna slices and sushi rice.
6. Arrange the Tuna Nigiri on a serving plate.
7. Serve the Tuna Nigiri with soy sauce, wasabi, and pickled ginger on the side.

Enjoy your homemade Tuna Nigiri!

Salmon Nigiri

Ingredients:

- Sushi-grade salmon
- Sushi rice (prepared with rice vinegar, sugar, and salt)
- Soy sauce, for serving
- Wasabi, for serving
- Pickled ginger, for serving

Instructions:

1. Start by preparing sushi rice according to package instructions. Once cooked, allow it to cool slightly before shaping into nigiri.
2. Slice the sushi-grade salmon into thin slices, approximately 1/4 inch thick and 1 inch wide. Use a sharp knife for clean cuts.
3. With wet hands, take a small amount of sushi rice and shape it into an oval or rectangular mound, about 1 inch in length and 1/2 inch in width.
4. Place a slice of salmon over the top of the rice mound, gently pressing down to adhere the salmon to the rice.
5. Repeat the process to make more nigiri, using up all the salmon slices and sushi rice.
6. Arrange the Salmon Nigiri on a serving plate.
7. Serve the Salmon Nigiri with soy sauce, wasabi, and pickled ginger on the side.

Enjoy your homemade Salmon Nigiri!

Yellowtail Nigiri

Ingredients:

- Sushi-grade yellowtail (also known as hamachi)
- Sushi rice (prepared with rice vinegar, sugar, and salt)
- Soy sauce, for serving
- Wasabi, for serving
- Pickled ginger, for serving

Instructions:

1. Start by preparing sushi rice according to package instructions. Once cooked, allow it to cool slightly before shaping into nigiri.
2. Slice the sushi-grade yellowtail into thin slices, approximately 1/4 inch thick and 1 inch wide. Use a sharp knife for clean cuts.
3. With wet hands, take a small amount of sushi rice and shape it into an oval or rectangular mound, about 1 inch in length and 1/2 inch in width.
4. Place a slice of yellowtail over the top of the rice mound, gently pressing down to adhere the yellowtail to the rice.
5. Repeat the process to make more nigiri, using up all the yellowtail slices and sushi rice.
6. Arrange the Yellowtail Nigiri on a serving plate.
7. Serve the Yellowtail Nigiri with soy sauce, wasabi, and pickled ginger on the side.

Enjoy your homemade Yellowtail Nigiri!

Eel Nigiri

Ingredients:

- Sushi-grade eel (unagi)
- Sushi rice (prepared with rice vinegar, sugar, and salt)
- Soy sauce, for serving
- Wasabi, for serving
- Pickled ginger, for serving

Instructions:

1. Begin by preparing sushi rice according to package instructions. Once cooked, allow it to cool slightly before shaping into nigiri.
2. If the eel is not pre-cooked, grill or broil the eel fillets until cooked through and slightly caramelized. Allow the eel to cool slightly before slicing.
3. Slice the sushi-grade eel into thin slices, approximately 1/4 inch thick and 1 inch wide. Use a sharp knife for clean cuts.
4. With wet hands, take a small amount of sushi rice and shape it into an oval or rectangular mound, about 1 inch in length and 1/2 inch in width.
5. Place a slice of eel over the top of the rice mound, gently pressing down to adhere the eel to the rice.
6. Repeat the process to make more nigiri, using up all the eel slices and sushi rice.
7. Optionally, brush the top of each eel nigiri with some eel sauce for added flavor and glossiness.
8. Arrange the Eel Nigiri on a serving plate.
9. Serve the Eel Nigiri with soy sauce, wasabi, and pickled ginger on the side.

Enjoy your homemade Eel Nigiri!

Shrimp Nigiri

Ingredients:

- Sushi-grade shrimp
- Sushi rice (prepared with rice vinegar, sugar, and salt)
- Soy sauce, for serving
- Wasabi, for serving
- Pickled ginger, for serving

Instructions:

1. Start by preparing sushi rice according to package instructions. Once cooked, let it cool slightly before shaping into nigiri.
2. Peel and devein the sushi-grade shrimp, leaving the tail intact if desired.
3. With wet hands, take a small amount of sushi rice and shape it into an oval or rectangular mound, about 1 inch in length and 1/2 inch in width.
4. Place one shrimp over the top of the rice mound, gently pressing down to adhere the shrimp to the rice.
5. Repeat the process to make more nigiri, using up all the shrimp and sushi rice.
6. Optionally, you can lightly sear or cook the shrimp before placing it on the rice if you prefer.
7. Arrange the Shrimp Nigiri on a serving plate.
8. Serve the Shrimp Nigiri with soy sauce, wasabi, and pickled ginger on the side.

Enjoy your homemade Shrimp Nigiri!

Scallop Nigiri

Ingredients:

- Sushi-grade scallops
- Sushi rice (prepared with rice vinegar, sugar, and salt)
- Soy sauce, for serving
- Wasabi, for serving
- Pickled ginger, for serving

Instructions:

1. Begin by preparing sushi rice according to package instructions. Once cooked, allow it to cool slightly before shaping into nigiri.
2. Rinse the sushi-grade scallops under cold water and pat them dry with paper towels.
3. With wet hands, take a small amount of sushi rice and shape it into an oval or rectangular mound, about 1 inch in length and 1/2 inch in width.
4. Place one scallop over the top of the rice mound, gently pressing down to adhere the scallop to the rice.
5. Repeat the process to make more nigiri, using up all the scallops and sushi rice.
6. Optionally, you can lightly sear the scallops before placing them on the rice if you prefer.
7. Arrange the Scallop Nigiri on a serving plate.
8. Serve the Scallop Nigiri with soy sauce, wasabi, and pickled ginger on the side.

Enjoy your homemade Scallop Nigiri!

Tamago Nigiri

Ingredients:

- 4 large eggs
- 2 tablespoons sugar
- 2 tablespoons mirin (Japanese sweet rice wine)
- 2 tablespoons soy sauce
- Vegetable oil for cooking
- Sushi rice (prepared with rice vinegar, sugar, and salt)
- Soy sauce, for serving
- Wasabi, for serving
- Pickled ginger, for serving

Instructions:

1. In a bowl, whisk together the eggs, sugar, mirin, and soy sauce until well combined.
2. Heat a small non-stick skillet over medium heat and lightly grease it with vegetable oil.
3. Pour a thin layer of the egg mixture into the skillet, just enough to cover the bottom. Cook until the edges start to set, then gently roll the egg from one side of the skillet to the other to create a thin omelette.
4. Once rolled, push the omelette to one side of the skillet and add a little more oil to the empty side. Pour another thin layer of the egg mixture into the empty side of the skillet and repeat the process of rolling the omelette.
5. Continue cooking and rolling the omelette until all the egg mixture is used up. You should end up with a thick rolled omelette.
6. Transfer the rolled omelette to a cutting board and slice it into equal-sized rectangles, approximately 1 inch wide and 2 inches long.
7. With wet hands, take a small amount of sushi rice and shape it into an oval or rectangular mound, about 1 inch in length and 1/2 inch in width.
8. Place one slice of tamago (rolled omelette) over the top of the rice mound, gently pressing down to adhere the tamago to the rice.
9. Repeat the process to make more nigiri, using up all the tamago slices and sushi rice.
10. Arrange the Tamago Nigiri on a serving plate.
11. Serve the Tamago Nigiri with soy sauce, wasabi, and pickled ginger on the side.

Enjoy your homemade Tamago Nigiri!

Octopus Nigiri

Ingredients:

- Sushi-grade octopus
- Sushi rice (prepared with rice vinegar, sugar, and salt)
- Soy sauce, for serving
- Wasabi, for serving
- Pickled ginger, for serving

Instructions:

1. Start by preparing sushi rice according to package instructions. Once cooked, let it cool slightly before shaping into nigiri.
2. If the octopus is not already cooked, simmer it in water with aromatics such as ginger, garlic, and green onions until tender, about 1-2 hours. Let it cool.
3. Slice the sushi-grade octopus into thin slices, approximately 1/4 inch thick and 1 inch wide.
4. With wet hands, take a small amount of sushi rice and shape it into an oval or rectangular mound, about 1 inch in length and 1/2 inch in width.
5. Place one slice of octopus over the top of the rice mound, gently pressing down to adhere the octopus to the rice.
6. Repeat the process to make more nigiri, using up all the octopus slices and sushi rice.
7. Arrange the Octopus Nigiri on a serving plate.
8. Serve the Octopus Nigiri with soy sauce, wasabi, and pickled ginger on the side.

Enjoy your homemade Octopus Nigiri!

Mackerel Nigiri

Ingredients:

- Sushi-grade mackerel fillets
- Sushi rice (prepared with rice vinegar, sugar, and salt)
- Soy sauce, for serving
- Wasabi, for serving
- Pickled ginger, for serving

Instructions:

1. Begin by preparing sushi rice according to package instructions. Once cooked, allow it to cool slightly before shaping into nigiri.
2. Rinse the sushi-grade mackerel fillets under cold water and pat them dry with paper towels.
3. Slice the mackerel fillets into thin slices, approximately 1/4 inch thick and 1 inch wide. Use a sharp knife for clean cuts.
4. With wet hands, take a small amount of sushi rice and shape it into an oval or rectangular mound, about 1 inch in length and 1/2 inch in width.
5. Place one slice of mackerel over the top of the rice mound, gently pressing down to adhere the mackerel to the rice.
6. Repeat the process to make more nigiri, using up all the mackerel slices and sushi rice.
7. Optionally, you can lightly sear the mackerel slices before placing them on the rice if you prefer.
8. Arrange the Mackerel Nigiri on a serving plate.
9. Serve the Mackerel Nigiri with soy sauce, wasabi, and pickled ginger on the side.

Enjoy your homemade Mackerel Nigiri!

Squid Nigiri

Ingredients:

- Sushi-grade squid
- Sushi rice (prepared with rice vinegar, sugar, and salt)
- Soy sauce, for serving
- Wasabi, for serving
- Pickled ginger, for serving

Instructions:

1. Start by preparing sushi rice according to package instructions. Once cooked, let it cool slightly before shaping into nigiri.
2. Rinse the sushi-grade squid under cold water and pat it dry with paper towels.
3. Slice the squid into thin slices, approximately 1/4 inch thick and 1 inch wide. Use a sharp knife for clean cuts.
4. With wet hands, take a small amount of sushi rice and shape it into an oval or rectangular mound, about 1 inch in length and 1/2 inch in width.
5. Place one slice of squid over the top of the rice mound, gently pressing down to adhere the squid to the rice.
6. Repeat the process to make more nigiri, using up all the squid slices and sushi rice.
7. Optionally, you can lightly grill or sear the squid slices before placing them on the rice if you prefer.
8. Arrange the Squid Nigiri on a serving plate.
9. Serve the Squid Nigiri with soy sauce, wasabi, and pickled ginger on the side.

Enjoy your homemade Squid Nigiri!

Surf and Turf Roll

Ingredients:

- 4 sheets nori seaweed
- 2 cups sushi rice
- 2 1/2 cups water
- 1/2 cup rice vinegar
- 2 tablespoons sugar
- 1 teaspoon salt
- 8 large shrimp, peeled and deveined
- 8 ounces sushi-grade beef (such as ribeye or filet mignon), thinly sliced
- 1/2 avocado, thinly sliced
- 1/2 cucumber, peeled, seeded, and cut into matchsticks
- Soy sauce, for serving
- Wasabi, for serving
- Pickled ginger, for serving
- Vegetable oil, for cooking

Instructions:

1. Rinse the sushi rice under cold water until the water runs clear. Cook the rice either in a rice cooker or on the stovetop according to the package instructions. Let it cool to room temperature.
2. In a small saucepan, combine the rice vinegar, sugar, and salt. Heat over medium heat until the sugar and salt dissolve. Remove from heat and let the mixture cool.
3. Once the rice is cooled, gently fold in the vinegar mixture until well combined. Set aside.
4. Heat a small amount of vegetable oil in a skillet over medium-high heat. Add the shrimp and cook for 2-3 minutes on each side until pink and opaque. Remove from the skillet and set aside.
5. In the same skillet, add the thinly sliced beef and cook for 1-2 minutes on each side until browned but still slightly pink in the center. Remove from the skillet and set aside.
6. Place a sheet of nori seaweed on a bamboo sushi mat, shiny side down. With wet hands, spread about 1/2 cup of sushi rice evenly over the nori, leaving a 1-inch border at the top edge.
7. Arrange slices of sushi-grade beef, avocado, cucumber matchsticks, and cooked shrimp across the center of the rice.

8. Roll the sushi tightly away from you using the bamboo mat, pressing gently to seal the edge. Dampen the top edge of the nori with a little water to help it stick.
9. Repeat the process with the remaining nori sheets and ingredients.
10. Using a sharp knife dipped in water, slice each roll into 6-8 pieces.
11. Serve the Surf and Turf Rolls with soy sauce, wasabi, and pickled ginger on the side.

Enjoy your homemade Surf and Turf Rolls!

Green Dragon Roll

Ingredients:

- 4 sheets nori seaweed
- 2 cups sushi rice
- 2 1/2 cups water
- 1/2 cup rice vinegar
- 2 tablespoons sugar
- 1 teaspoon salt
- 1 avocado
- 8 large shrimp, cooked and peeled
- 4 ounces sushi-grade tuna or salmon, thinly sliced
- 1/2 cucumber, peeled, seeded, and cut into matchsticks
- Soy sauce, for serving
- Wasabi, for serving
- Pickled ginger, for serving

Instructions:

1. Rinse the sushi rice under cold water until the water runs clear. Cook the rice either in a rice cooker or on the stovetop according to the package instructions. Let it cool to room temperature.
2. In a small saucepan, combine the rice vinegar, sugar, and salt. Heat over medium heat until the sugar and salt dissolve. Remove from heat and let the mixture cool.
3. Once the rice is cooled, gently fold in the vinegar mixture until well combined. Set aside.
4. Peel and slice the avocado into thin strips.
5. Place a sheet of nori seaweed on a bamboo sushi mat, shiny side down. With wet hands, spread about 1/2 cup of sushi rice evenly over the nori, leaving a 1-inch border at the top edge.
6. Arrange slices of avocado, cooked shrimp, sushi-grade tuna or salmon, and cucumber matchsticks across the center of the rice.
7. Roll the sushi tightly away from you using the bamboo mat, pressing gently to seal the edge. Dampen the top edge of the nori with a little water to help it stick.
8. Using a sharp knife dipped in water, slice the roll into 8 equal pieces.
9. Arrange the Green Dragon Roll pieces on a serving platter.
10. Serve with soy sauce, wasabi, and pickled ginger on the side.

Enjoy your homemade Green Dragon Roll!

Rainbow Dragon Roll

Ingredients:

- 4 sheets nori seaweed
- 2 cups sushi rice
- 2 1/2 cups water
- 1/2 cup rice vinegar
- 2 tablespoons sugar
- 1 teaspoon salt
- 8 large shrimp, cooked and peeled
- 4 ounces sushi-grade tuna, thinly sliced
- 4 ounces sushi-grade salmon, thinly sliced
- 1/2 avocado
- 1/2 cucumber, peeled, seeded, and cut into matchsticks
- Soy sauce, for serving
- Wasabi, for serving
- Pickled ginger, for serving

Instructions:

1. Rinse the sushi rice under cold water until the water runs clear. Cook the rice either in a rice cooker or on the stovetop according to the package instructions. Let it cool to room temperature.
2. In a small saucepan, combine the rice vinegar, sugar, and salt. Heat over medium heat until the sugar and salt dissolve. Remove from heat and let the mixture cool.
3. Once the rice is cooled, gently fold in the vinegar mixture until well combined. Set aside.
4. Peel and slice the avocado into thin strips.
5. Place a sheet of nori seaweed on a bamboo sushi mat, shiny side down. With wet hands, spread about 1/2 cup of sushi rice evenly over the nori, leaving a 1-inch border at the top edge.
6. Arrange slices of avocado and cucumber matchsticks across the center of the rice.
7. Roll the sushi tightly away from you using the bamboo mat, pressing gently to seal the edge. Dampen the top edge of the nori with a little water to help it stick.
8. Place the cooked shrimp on top of the rolled sushi, arranging them in a row along the length of the roll.

9. Place slices of sushi-grade tuna on top of the shrimp, followed by slices of sushi-grade salmon.
10. Using a sharp knife dipped in water, slice the roll into 8 equal pieces.
11. Arrange the Rainbow Dragon Roll pieces on a serving platter.
12. Serve with soy sauce, wasabi, and pickled ginger on the side.

Enjoy your homemade Rainbow Dragon Roll, a visually stunning and delicious treat!

Sunrise Roll

Ingredients:

- 4 sheets nori seaweed
- 2 cups sushi rice
- 2 1/2 cups water
- 1/2 cup rice vinegar
- 2 tablespoons sugar
- 1 teaspoon salt
- 8 large shrimp, cooked and peeled
- 1 ripe mango, thinly sliced
- 1 ripe avocado, thinly sliced
- 4 ounces sushi-grade tuna or salmon, thinly sliced
- Soy sauce, for serving
- Wasabi, for serving
- Pickled ginger, for serving

Instructions:

1. Rinse the sushi rice under cold water until the water runs clear. Cook the rice either in a rice cooker or on the stovetop according to the package instructions. Let it cool to room temperature.
2. In a small saucepan, combine the rice vinegar, sugar, and salt. Heat over medium heat until the sugar and salt dissolve. Remove from heat and let the mixture cool.
3. Once the rice is cooled, gently fold in the vinegar mixture until well combined. Set aside.
4. Place a sheet of nori seaweed on a bamboo sushi mat, shiny side down. With wet hands, spread about 1/2 cup of sushi rice evenly over the nori, leaving a 1-inch border at the top edge.
5. Arrange slices of mango and avocado across the center of the rice.
6. Roll the sushi tightly away from you using the bamboo mat, pressing gently to seal the edge. Dampen the top edge of the nori with a little water to help it stick.
7. Place the cooked shrimp on top of the rolled sushi, arranging them in a row along the length of the roll.
8. Place slices of sushi-grade tuna or salmon on top of the shrimp.
9. Using a sharp knife dipped in water, slice the roll into 8 equal pieces.
10. Arrange the Sunrise Roll pieces on a serving platter.
11. Serve with soy sauce, wasabi, and pickled ginger on the side.

Enjoy your homemade Sunrise Roll, a delightful blend of sweet and savory flavors!

Sunset Roll

Ingredients:

- 4 sheets nori seaweed
- 2 cups sushi rice
- 2 1/2 cups water
- 1/2 cup rice vinegar
- 2 tablespoons sugar
- 1 teaspoon salt
- 8 large shrimp, cooked and peeled
- 1 ripe mango, thinly sliced
- 1 ripe avocado, thinly sliced
- 4 ounces sushi-grade salmon, thinly sliced
- 1/2 cucumber, peeled, seeded, and cut into matchsticks
- Soy sauce, for serving
- Wasabi, for serving
- Pickled ginger, for serving

Instructions:

1. Rinse the sushi rice under cold water until the water runs clear. Cook the rice either in a rice cooker or on the stovetop according to the package instructions. Let it cool to room temperature.
2. In a small saucepan, combine the rice vinegar, sugar, and salt. Heat over medium heat until the sugar and salt dissolve. Remove from heat and let the mixture cool.
3. Once the rice is cooled, gently fold in the vinegar mixture until well combined. Set aside.
4. Place a sheet of nori seaweed on a bamboo sushi mat, shiny side down. With wet hands, spread about 1/2 cup of sushi rice evenly over the nori, leaving a 1-inch border at the top edge.
5. Arrange slices of mango, avocado, cucumber matchsticks, and sushi-grade salmon across the center of the rice.
6. Roll the sushi tightly away from you using the bamboo mat, pressing gently to seal the edge. Dampen the top edge of the nori with a little water to help it stick.
7. Place the cooked shrimp on top of the rolled sushi, arranging them in a row along the length of the roll.
8. Using a sharp knife dipped in water, slice the roll into 8 equal pieces.
9. Arrange the Sunset Roll pieces on a serving platter.

10. Serve with soy sauce, wasabi, and pickled ginger on the side.

Enjoy your homemade Sunset Roll, a delightful combination of flavors and colors reminiscent of a beautiful sunset!

Firecracker Roll

Ingredients:

- 4 sheets nori seaweed
- 2 cups sushi rice
- 2 1/2 cups water
- 1/2 cup rice vinegar
- 2 tablespoons sugar
- 1 teaspoon salt
- 8 large shrimp, cooked and peeled
- 4 ounces sushi-grade tuna or salmon, thinly sliced
- 1/2 avocado, thinly sliced
- 1/4 cup spicy mayonnaise (mix mayonnaise with Sriracha sauce to taste)
- 1/4 cup crunchy tempura flakes
- Soy sauce, for serving
- Wasabi, for serving
- Pickled ginger, for serving

Instructions:

1. Rinse the sushi rice under cold water until the water runs clear. Cook the rice either in a rice cooker or on the stovetop according to the package instructions. Let it cool to room temperature.
2. In a small saucepan, combine the rice vinegar, sugar, and salt. Heat over medium heat until the sugar and salt dissolve. Remove from heat and let the mixture cool.
3. Once the rice is cooled, gently fold in the vinegar mixture until well combined. Set aside.
4. Place a sheet of nori seaweed on a bamboo sushi mat, shiny side down. With wet hands, spread about 1/2 cup of sushi rice evenly over the nori, leaving a 1-inch border at the top edge.
5. Spread a thin layer of spicy mayonnaise over the rice.
6. Arrange slices of avocado and sushi-grade tuna or salmon across the center of the rice.
7. Roll the sushi tightly away from you using the bamboo mat, pressing gently to seal the edge. Dampen the top edge of the nori with a little water to help it stick.
8. Place the cooked shrimp on top of the rolled sushi, arranging them in a row along the length of the roll.

9. Sprinkle crunchy tempura flakes over the top of the roll.
10. Using a sharp knife dipped in water, slice the roll into 8 equal pieces.
11. Arrange the Firecracker Roll pieces on a serving platter.
12. Serve with soy sauce, wasabi, and pickled ginger on the side.

Enjoy your homemade Firecracker Roll, a spicy and crunchy delight!

Dynamite Crunch Roll

Ingredients:

- 4 sheets nori seaweed
- 2 cups sushi rice
- 2 1/2 cups water
- 1/2 cup rice vinegar
- 2 tablespoons sugar
- 1 teaspoon salt
- 8 large shrimp, cooked and peeled
- 1/2 avocado, thinly sliced
- 1/4 cup spicy mayonnaise (mix mayonnaise with Sriracha sauce to taste)
- 1/4 cup crunchy tempura flakes
- Soy sauce, for serving
- Wasabi, for serving
- Pickled ginger, for serving

Instructions:

1. Rinse the sushi rice under cold water until the water runs clear. Cook the rice either in a rice cooker or on the stovetop according to the package instructions. Let it cool to room temperature.
2. In a small saucepan, combine the rice vinegar, sugar, and salt. Heat over medium heat until the sugar and salt dissolve. Remove from heat and let the mixture cool.
3. Once the rice is cooled, gently fold in the vinegar mixture until well combined. Set aside.
4. Place a sheet of nori seaweed on a bamboo sushi mat, shiny side down. With wet hands, spread about 1/2 cup of sushi rice evenly over the nori, leaving a 1-inch border at the top edge.
5. Spread a thin layer of spicy mayonnaise over the rice.
6. Arrange slices of avocado and cooked shrimp across the center of the rice.
7. Roll the sushi tightly away from you using the bamboo mat, pressing gently to seal the edge. Dampen the top edge of the nori with a little water to help it stick.
8. Sprinkle crunchy tempura flakes over the top of the roll.
9. Using a sharp knife dipped in water, slice the roll into 8 equal pieces.
10. Arrange the Dynamite Crunch Roll pieces on a serving platter.
11. Serve with soy sauce, wasabi, and pickled ginger on the side.

Enjoy your homemade Dynamite Crunch Roll, a delicious and satisfying treat!

Panko Crusted Roll

Ingredients:

- 4 sheets nori seaweed
- 2 cups sushi rice
- 2 1/2 cups water
- 1/2 cup rice vinegar
- 2 tablespoons sugar
- 1 teaspoon salt
- 8 large shrimp, cooked and peeled
- 1/2 avocado, thinly sliced
- 1/4 cup spicy mayonnaise (mix mayonnaise with Sriracha sauce to taste)
- 1/4 cup panko breadcrumbs
- Vegetable oil for frying
- Soy sauce, for serving
- Wasabi, for serving
- Pickled ginger, for serving

Instructions:

1. Rinse the sushi rice under cold water until the water runs clear. Cook the rice either in a rice cooker or on the stovetop according to the package instructions. Let it cool to room temperature.
2. In a small saucepan, combine the rice vinegar, sugar, and salt. Heat over medium heat until the sugar and salt dissolve. Remove from heat and let the mixture cool.
3. Once the rice is cooled, gently fold in the vinegar mixture until well combined. Set aside.
4. Place a sheet of nori seaweed on a bamboo sushi mat, shiny side down. With wet hands, spread about 1/2 cup of sushi rice evenly over the nori, leaving a 1-inch border at the top edge.
5. Spread a thin layer of spicy mayonnaise over the rice.
6. Arrange slices of avocado and cooked shrimp across the center of the rice.
7. Roll the sushi tightly away from you using the bamboo mat, pressing gently to seal the edge. Dampen the top edge of the nori with a little water to help it stick.
8. Heat vegetable oil in a pan over medium heat. While the oil is heating, roll the sushi roll in panko breadcrumbs, making sure to coat all sides evenly.

9. Once the oil is hot, carefully place the panko-crusted sushi roll in the pan and fry until the panko is golden brown and crispy on all sides, turning occasionally. This should take about 2-3 minutes.
10. Remove the roll from the pan and place it on a cutting board. Using a sharp knife dipped in water, slice the roll into 8 equal pieces.
11. Arrange the Panko Crusted Roll pieces on a serving platter.
12. Serve with soy sauce, wasabi, and pickled ginger on the side.

Enjoy your homemade Panko Crusted Roll, a crunchy and flavorful twist on traditional sushi!

Tuna Tataki Roll

Ingredients:

- 4 sheets nori seaweed
- 2 cups sushi rice
- 2 1/2 cups water
- 1/2 cup rice vinegar
- 2 tablespoons sugar
- 1 teaspoon salt
- 8 ounces sushi-grade tuna loin
- 1/4 cup sesame seeds
- 1 tablespoon vegetable oil
- Soy sauce, for serving
- Wasabi, for serving
- Pickled ginger, for serving

Instructions:

1. Rinse the sushi rice under cold water until the water runs clear. Cook the rice either in a rice cooker or on the stovetop according to the package instructions. Let it cool to room temperature.
2. In a small saucepan, combine the rice vinegar, sugar, and salt. Heat over medium heat until the sugar and salt dissolve. Remove from heat and let the mixture cool.
3. Once the rice is cooled, gently fold in the vinegar mixture until well combined. Set aside.
4. Heat a skillet over high heat. While the skillet is heating, coat the tuna loin with sesame seeds, pressing gently to adhere.
5. Add vegetable oil to the skillet. Once hot, sear the tuna loin for about 30 seconds to 1 minute on each side, or until the sesame seeds are lightly toasted. The tuna should still be rare in the center. Remove from heat and let it cool slightly before slicing.
6. Slice the seared tuna loin into thin slices.
7. Place a sheet of nori seaweed on a bamboo sushi mat, shiny side down. With wet hands, spread about 1/2 cup of sushi rice evenly over the nori, leaving a 1-inch border at the top edge.
8. Arrange slices of seared tuna across the center of the rice.

9. Roll the sushi tightly away from you using the bamboo mat, pressing gently to seal the edge. Dampen the top edge of the nori with a little water to help it stick.
10. Using a sharp knife dipped in water, slice the roll into 8 equal pieces.
11. Arrange the Tuna Tataki Roll pieces on a serving platter.
12. Serve with soy sauce, wasabi, and pickled ginger on the side.

Enjoy your homemade Tuna Tataki Roll, featuring deliciously seared tuna and sushi rice!

Seared Salmon Roll

Ingredients:

- 4 sheets nori seaweed
- 2 cups sushi rice
- 2 1/2 cups water
- 1/2 cup rice vinegar
- 2 tablespoons sugar
- 1 teaspoon salt
- 8 ounces sushi-grade salmon fillet
- Soy sauce, for serving
- Wasabi, for serving
- Pickled ginger, for serving
- Vegetable oil, for searing

Instructions:

1. Rinse the sushi rice under cold water until the water runs clear. Cook the rice either in a rice cooker or on the stovetop according to the package instructions. Let it cool to room temperature.
2. In a small saucepan, combine the rice vinegar, sugar, and salt. Heat over medium heat until the sugar and salt dissolve. Remove from heat and let the mixture cool.
3. Once the rice is cooled, gently fold in the vinegar mixture until well combined. Set aside.
4. Cut the salmon fillet into thin slices.
5. Heat a small amount of vegetable oil in a skillet over medium-high heat. When the skillet is hot, add the salmon slices and sear them for about 30 seconds to 1 minute on each side, or until the salmon is lightly browned on the outside and still slightly rare in the center. Remove from heat and let it cool slightly.
6. Place a sheet of nori seaweed on a bamboo sushi mat, shiny side down. With wet hands, spread about 1/2 cup of sushi rice evenly over the nori, leaving a 1-inch border at the top edge.
7. Arrange slices of seared salmon across the center of the rice.
8. Roll the sushi tightly away from you using the bamboo mat, pressing gently to seal the edge. Dampen the top edge of the nori with a little water to help it stick.
9. Using a sharp knife dipped in water, slice the roll into 8 equal pieces.
10. Arrange the Seared Salmon Roll pieces on a serving platter.

11. Serve with soy sauce, wasabi, and pickled ginger on the side.

Enjoy your homemade Seared Salmon Roll, featuring succulent seared salmon and perfectly seasoned sushi rice!

Avocado Cucumber Roll

Ingredients:

- 4 sheets nori seaweed
- 2 cups sushi rice
- 2 1/2 cups water
- 1/2 cup rice vinegar
- 2 tablespoons sugar
- 1 teaspoon salt
- 1 ripe avocado, sliced
- 1/2 cucumber, peeled and cut into thin strips
- Soy sauce, for serving
- Wasabi, for serving
- Pickled ginger, for serving

Instructions:

1. Rinse the sushi rice under cold water until the water runs clear. Cook the rice either in a rice cooker or on the stovetop according to the package instructions. Let it cool to room temperature.
2. In a small saucepan, combine the rice vinegar, sugar, and salt. Heat over medium heat until the sugar and salt dissolve. Remove from heat and let the mixture cool.
3. Once the rice is cooled, gently fold in the vinegar mixture until well combined. Set aside.
4. Place a sheet of nori seaweed on a bamboo sushi mat, shiny side down. With wet hands, spread about 1/2 cup of sushi rice evenly over the nori, leaving a 1-inch border at the top edge.
5. Arrange slices of avocado and cucumber strips across the center of the rice.
6. Roll the sushi tightly away from you using the bamboo mat, pressing gently to seal the edge. Dampen the top edge of the nori with a little water to help it stick.
7. Using a sharp knife dipped in water, slice the roll into 8 equal pieces.
8. Arrange the Avocado Cucumber Roll pieces on a serving platter.
9. Serve with soy sauce, wasabi, and pickled ginger on the side.

Enjoy your homemade Avocado Cucumber Roll, a refreshing and healthy sushi option!

Tofu Roll

Ingredients:

- 4 sheets nori seaweed
- 2 cups sushi rice
- 2 1/2 cups water
- 1/2 cup rice vinegar
- 2 tablespoons sugar
- 1 teaspoon salt
- 1 block firm tofu, sliced into thin strips
- Soy sauce, for marinating tofu and serving
- 1 tablespoon vegetable oil
- 1/2 cucumber, peeled and cut into thin strips
- 1/2 avocado, sliced
- Soy sauce, for serving
- Wasabi, for serving
- Pickled ginger, for serving

Instructions:

1. Rinse the sushi rice under cold water until the water runs clear. Cook the rice either in a rice cooker or on the stovetop according to the package instructions. Let it cool to room temperature.
2. In a small saucepan, combine the rice vinegar, sugar, and salt. Heat over medium heat until the sugar and salt dissolve. Remove from heat and let the mixture cool.
3. Once the rice is cooled, gently fold in the vinegar mixture until well combined. Set aside.
4. Marinate the tofu strips in soy sauce for about 15-30 minutes.
5. Heat vegetable oil in a skillet over medium-high heat. Add the marinated tofu strips and cook until golden brown on both sides, about 3-4 minutes per side. Remove from heat and let it cool slightly.
6. Place a sheet of nori seaweed on a bamboo sushi mat, shiny side down. With wet hands, spread about 1/2 cup of sushi rice evenly over the nori, leaving a 1-inch border at the top edge.
7. Arrange slices of avocado, cucumber strips, and cooked tofu across the center of the rice.

8. Roll the sushi tightly away from you using the bamboo mat, pressing gently to seal the edge. Dampen the top edge of the nori with a little water to help it stick.
9. Using a sharp knife dipped in water, slice the roll into 8 equal pieces.
10. Arrange the Tofu Roll pieces on a serving platter.
11. Serve with soy sauce, wasabi, and pickled ginger on the side.

Enjoy your homemade Tofu Roll, a delicious and vegetarian-friendly sushi option!

Kimchi Roll

Ingredients:

- 4 sheets nori seaweed
- 2 cups sushi rice
- 2 1/2 cups water
- 1/2 cup rice vinegar
- 2 tablespoons sugar
- 1 teaspoon salt
- 1 cup kimchi, drained and thinly sliced
- 1/2 cucumber, peeled and cut into thin strips
- 1/2 avocado, sliced
- Soy sauce, for serving
- Wasabi, for serving
- Pickled ginger, for serving

Instructions:

1. Rinse the sushi rice under cold water until the water runs clear. Cook the rice either in a rice cooker or on the stovetop according to the package instructions. Let it cool to room temperature.
2. In a small saucepan, combine the rice vinegar, sugar, and salt. Heat over medium heat until the sugar and salt dissolve. Remove from heat and let the mixture cool.
3. Once the rice is cooled, gently fold in the vinegar mixture until well combined. Set aside.
4. Place a sheet of nori seaweed on a bamboo sushi mat, shiny side down. With wet hands, spread about 1/2 cup of sushi rice evenly over the nori, leaving a 1-inch border at the top edge.
5. Arrange slices of avocado, cucumber strips, and kimchi across the center of the rice.
6. Roll the sushi tightly away from you using the bamboo mat, pressing gently to seal the edge. Dampen the top edge of the nori with a little water to help it stick.
7. Using a sharp knife dipped in water, slice the roll into 8 equal pieces.
8. Arrange the Kimchi Roll pieces on a serving platter.
9. Serve with soy sauce, wasabi, and pickled ginger on the side.

Enjoy your homemade Kimchi Roll, a flavorful and unique twist on traditional sushi!

Pickled Radish Roll

Ingredients:

- 4 sheets nori seaweed
- 2 cups sushi rice
- 2 1/2 cups water
- 1/2 cup rice vinegar
- 2 tablespoons sugar
- 1 teaspoon salt
- 1 cup pickled radish (Danmuji), thinly sliced
- 1/2 cucumber, peeled and cut into thin strips
- Soy sauce, for serving
- Wasabi, for serving
- Pickled ginger, for serving

Instructions:

1. Rinse the sushi rice under cold water until the water runs clear. Cook the rice either in a rice cooker or on the stovetop according to the package instructions. Let it cool to room temperature.
2. In a small saucepan, combine the rice vinegar, sugar, and salt. Heat over medium heat until the sugar and salt dissolve. Remove from heat and let the mixture cool.
3. Once the rice is cooled, gently fold in the vinegar mixture until well combined. Set aside.
4. Place a sheet of nori seaweed on a bamboo sushi mat, shiny side down. With wet hands, spread about 1/2 cup of sushi rice evenly over the nori, leaving a 1-inch border at the top edge.
5. Arrange slices of pickled radish and cucumber strips across the center of the rice.
6. Roll the sushi tightly away from you using the bamboo mat, pressing gently to seal the edge. Dampen the top edge of the nori with a little water to help it stick.
7. Using a sharp knife dipped in water, slice the roll into 8 equal pieces.
8. Arrange the Pickled Radish Roll pieces on a serving platter.
9. Serve with soy sauce, wasabi, and pickled ginger on the side.

Enjoy your homemade Pickled Radish Roll, a refreshing and tangy sushi option!

Quinoa Roll

Ingredients:

- 1 cup sushi rice
- 1 1/4 cups water
- 2 tablespoons rice vinegar
- 1 tablespoon sugar
- 1 teaspoon salt
- 4 sheets nori seaweed
- 1 cup cooked quinoa
- 1/2 cucumber, peeled and cut into thin strips
- 1/2 avocado, sliced
- Soy sauce, for serving
- Wasabi, for serving
- Pickled ginger, for serving

Instructions:

1. Rinse the sushi rice under cold water until the water runs clear. Combine the rice and water in a rice cooker or pot and cook according to the package instructions.
2. In a small saucepan, combine the rice vinegar, sugar, and salt. Heat over medium heat until the sugar and salt dissolve. Remove from heat and let the mixture cool.
3. Once the rice is cooked, transfer it to a large bowl and gently fold in the vinegar mixture until well combined. Let the rice cool to room temperature.
4. Place a sheet of nori seaweed on a bamboo sushi mat, shiny side down. With wet hands, spread a thin layer of cooked quinoa evenly over the nori, leaving a 1-inch border at the top edge.
5. Arrange slices of avocado and cucumber strips across the center of the quinoa.
6. Roll the sushi tightly away from you using the bamboo mat, pressing gently to seal the edge. Dampen the top edge of the nori with a little water to help it stick.
7. Using a sharp knife dipped in water, slice the roll into 8 equal pieces.
8. Arrange the Quinoa Roll pieces on a serving platter.
9. Serve with soy sauce, wasabi, and pickled ginger on the side.

Enjoy your homemade Quinoa Roll, a nutritious and delicious twist on traditional sushi!

Sashimi Salad Roll

Ingredients:

- 4 sheets nori seaweed
- 2 cups sushi rice
- 2 1/2 cups water
- 1/2 cup rice vinegar
- 2 tablespoons sugar
- 1 teaspoon salt
- Assorted sashimi (such as tuna, salmon, yellowtail), thinly sliced
- Mixed salad greens
- 1/2 cucumber, julienned
- 1/2 avocado, sliced
- Soy sauce, for serving
- Wasabi, for serving
- Pickled ginger, for serving

Instructions:

1. Rinse the sushi rice under cold water until the water runs clear. Cook the rice either in a rice cooker or on the stovetop according to the package instructions. Let it cool to room temperature.
2. In a small saucepan, combine the rice vinegar, sugar, and salt. Heat over medium heat until the sugar and salt dissolve. Remove from heat and let the mixture cool.
3. Once the rice is cooled, gently fold in the vinegar mixture until well combined. Set aside.
4. Place a sheet of nori seaweed on a bamboo sushi mat, shiny side down. With wet hands, spread about 1/2 cup of sushi rice evenly over the nori, leaving a 1-inch border at the top edge.
5. Arrange a layer of mixed salad greens, cucumber strips, avocado slices, and assorted sashimi across the center of the rice.
6. Roll the sushi tightly away from you using the bamboo mat, pressing gently to seal the edge. Dampen the top edge of the nori with a little water to help it stick.
7. Using a sharp knife dipped in water, slice the roll into 8 equal pieces.
8. Arrange the Sashimi Salad Roll pieces on a serving platter.
9. Serve with soy sauce, wasabi, and pickled ginger on the side.

Enjoy your homemade Sashimi Salad Roll, a refreshing and colorful sushi option!

www.ingramcontent.com/pod-product-compliance
Lightning Source LLC
LaVergne TN
LVHW081612060526
838201LV00054B/2221